HELLO NEIC:

WE ARE LETA & NIA TAYLOR

WE CREATED THIS BOOK TOGETHER AS A MOTHER/DAUGHTER COLLABORATION TO SHARE OUR DEEP APPRECIATION OF NATURE AND ART.

OUR INTENTION FOR THIS BOOK IS TO SHOW OUR LOVE AND SUPPORT FOR THIS COMMUNITY BY CREATING A CHILDREN'S BOOK WHERE A PORTION OF THE PROCEEDS WILL GO TO VARIED LOCAL CONSERVATION EFFORTS.

COCHRANE IS MY HOME
COPYRIGHT © 2022 BY LETA TAYLOR & NIA TAYLOR
ALL RIGHTS RESERVED
NO PART OF THIS BOOK MAY BE USED OR REPRODUCED IN ANY MANNER WHATSOEVER WITHOUT WRITTEN PERMISSION
FOR MORE INFORMATION, EMAIL THE AUTHOR

COVER CREATED BY LETA TAYLOR (WWW.SPACESOFARCADIA.COM)
LAYOUT BY RYAN DONNELLY

EMAIL LETA3006@YAHOO.COM
INSTAGRAM @SPACESOFARCADIA

COCHRANE

IS MY

HOME

WHAT IS IN THE DEN?

THE HUNGRY BEAR

WHAT IS IN THE SKY?

THE NORTHERN LIGHTS

WHAT IS BY THE FARM?

THE FLUFFY COW

WHAT IS IN THE FIELD?

THE PLAYFUL DEER

WHERE CAN WE HIKE?

IN THE FOREST

WHAT IS ON THE HILL?

THE HOPPING HARE

WHAT IS OUT AT NIGHT?

THE CLEVER FOX

WHAT BLOOMS IN THE SPRING?

WILDFLOWERS

WHAT IS IN THE VALLEY?

THE MAJESTIC MOOSE

WHAT HUGS COCHRANE?

THE BEAUTIFUL ROCKY MOUNTAINS

WHERE DO I LIVE?

COCHRANE
THIS IS MY HOME

SPACES OF ARCADIA

Manufactured by Amazon.ca
Bolton, ON